South Carolina's Beautiful Foothills Trail

SUCCESS ON THE FOOTHILLS TRAIL

By Richard T. Monahan

SUCCESS ON THE FOOTHILLS TRAIL

It's all about the Journey

Written by Richard T. Monahan

Copyright ©2018 by Richard T. Monahan All rights reserved. This book or any portion thereof may not be reproduced or used in any manner whatsoever without the express written permission of the publisher except for the use of brief quotations in a book review.

Cover design photographs, and images by Richard T. Monahan

Email contact: r.monahan@ymail.com

Second Printing 2018

ISBN-13
978-1986984881

ISBN-10
1986984885

Contents

Dedication	v
Acknowledgment	vii
Map	ix
CHAPTER ONE ◇ THE FOOTHILLS TRAIL	1
CHAPTER TWO ◇ THE FIRST TWO ATTEMPTS	3
CHAPTER THREE ◇ THE THIRD TIME IS A CHARM	7
CHAPTER FOUR ◇ LESSONS LEARNED ON THE FOOTHILL TRAIL	15
FOOTHILLS TRAIL ◇ PICTURES	16
ABOUT THE AUTHOR	51

DEDICATION

This book is dedicated to my father, Thomas P. Monahan, who always encouraged me to achieve all my desired goals. My father passed away at the age of 78 years old. I am happy, honored, and proud to do this hike at my age of 78 years old in his memory.

ACKNOWLEDGMENT

My special thanks to my friend and former co-worker Ronald K. Lai for being my editor. Once again he has used his command of the English language and grammar to take my words and present them in a format that is both interesting to read, and in the correct syntax and grammar.

Foothills National Recreation Trail

Located in northwestern Foothills of South Carolina

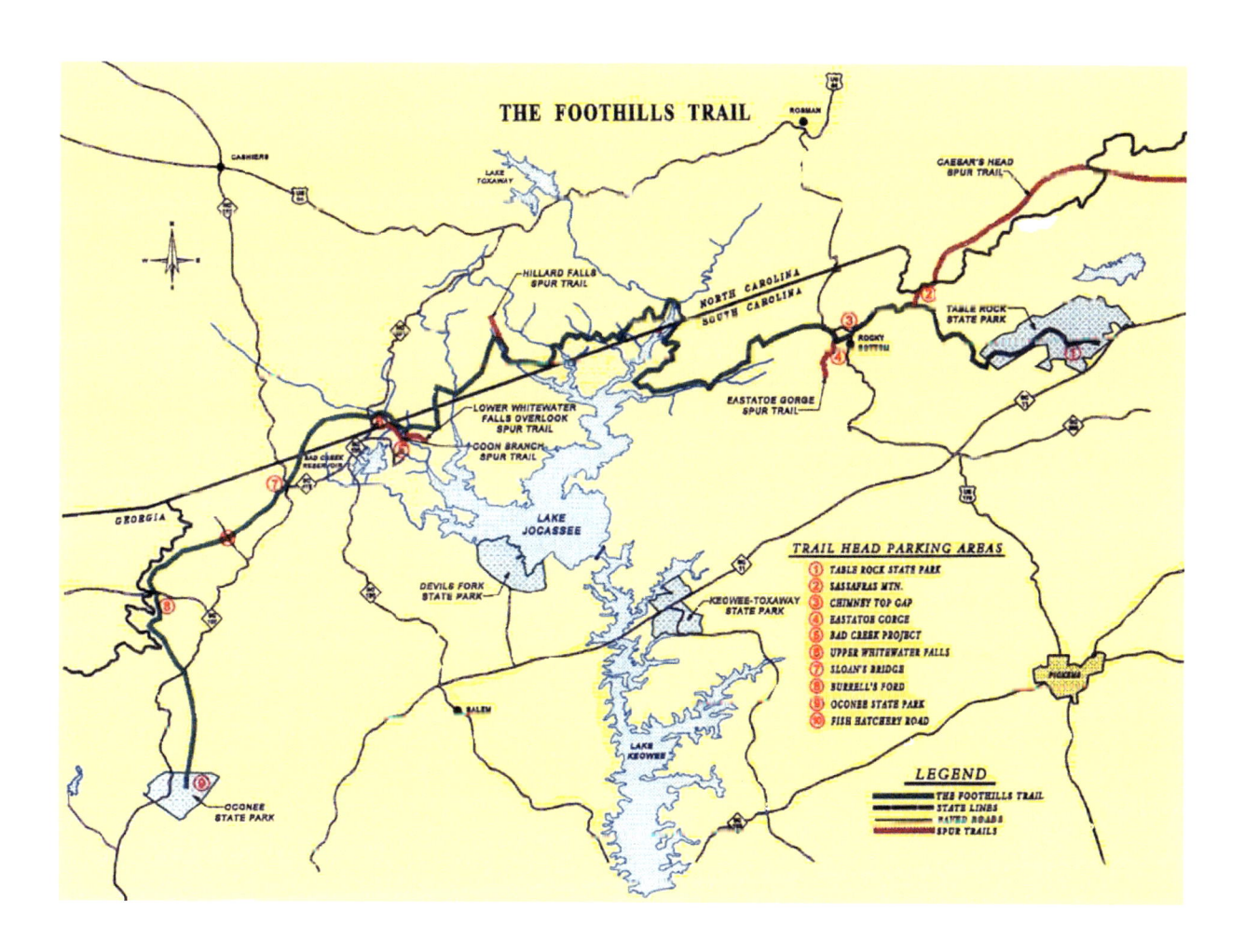

CHAPTER ONE – THE FOOTHILLS TRAIL

The Foothills Trail was first conceived in the 1960's. Clemson University's Recreation & Park Administration Department and the U.S. Forest Service initiated the development of the Foothills Trail. In the 1970's there were significant gains constructing many parts of the Trail. The 76.2 mile trail linking the Oconee and the Table Rock State Parks was in place by 1981. The Foothills Trail Conference was established in 1974 as a nonprofit organization to promote, support and oversee maintenance of this trail. This Trail offers a rugged backcountry experience for thru-hikers who will encounter strenuous hiking each day. Water sources and established campsites are plentiful all along the Trail. The average thru-hike takes between 5 to 6 days to complete the Trail, and the most preferred hiking season is in the fall.

I first discovered the existence of the Foothills Trail while researching long distance hiking trails on the internet. I am a residence of South Carolina and was very attracted by the existence of this hiking trail in my home state. The Foothills Trail is a hiking footpath that begins and ends in South Carolina crossing into North Carolina twice between its western terminus at the Oconee State Park and its eastern terminus at the Table Rock State Park. The Trail passes over the Sassafras Mountain, South Carolina's highest point at 3,553 feet above sea level. The prime trail scenic landscape is located in the Blue Ridge Mountains Range, passing over many streams, and engorged rivers with small, sandy beaches. The Trail skirts the beautiful Lake Jocassee and crosses the Chattaoga River, the Whitewater River, the Thomason River, the Horsepasture River, and the Toxaway River. It passes the Licklog Falls, the King Creek Falls, the Whitewater Falls (the highest waterfall east of the Mississippi), the Hilliard Falls, the Laurel Fork Falls, and the Virginia Hawkins Falls. There is a lot to be fond of about this Trail, located mostly in the wilderness. Besides having abundant camping opportunities and water sources along the entire length of the Trail, it has multiple suspension bridges and wooden bridges, many ascents and descents that are lined with wooden steps and many swimming opportunities in the warmer months. The path is well-marked with 2 X 6 inch white blazes and has elevation changes between 1100 and 3553 feet.

CHAPTER TWO – THE FIRST TWO ATTEMPTS

During the past year and a half I have made three attempts to thru-hike the Foothills Trail. My first two attempts ended before completion. My third attempt was a successful thru-hike of the Foothills Trail. Before beginning my first hike, I mentioned the trek to my good friend, Jim Davis, who lives on the Eastern Shore of Virginia. He asked me if he could join me. I have usually carried out all my long distance hiking by myself for several personal reasons; but, on this occasion, I relented and told Jim to join me.

…..On Sunday, May 22, 2016 Jim and I began our thru-hike of the Foothills Trail at the western terminus in the Oconee State Park. During the afternoon of the second day, Jim slowed his hiking pace down and complained that he had leg cramps and low blood sugar level. On day three Jim did not eat any dinner and said he had stomach pain. On Thursday, the fourth day, Jim felt very nauseous and once again did not eat dinner. The following day we only hiked 7.1 miles to the Laurel Forks Campground where we decided to camp for the night. Jim said he was tired and laid down for an afternoon nap. That evening Jim did eat dinner and said he felt a little better. We discussed ending our hike at the next trail access. The following morning Jim decided to call Jim Simpson our shuttle driver and arrange for a ride from SC178 parking lot back to our car at Table Rock State Park. We ate breakfast and prepared to leave camp. Our hike out this morning was about seven miles. At 1 p.m. we arrived at the parking lot where Jim Simpson was waiting for us to drive us back to our car. On the way home Jim seemed to improve very fast, and he said he felt much better.

We had completed 62 miles of the Foothills Trail. We never found out exactly what caused Jim's ailment but surmised that the water he was drinking did not agree with him. Although I was drinking the same filtered water as Jim, and I felt fine.

On Thursday, October 20, 2016, I once again set out to thru-hike the Foothills Trail. Several days prior to leaving for the trail my wife was bitten by fire ants, resulting in a very allergic reaction, consequentially breaking out in hives and a rash. She went to the Emergency Room and received an epee pen and a Benadryl injection. The next day she felt much better. On the morning of October 20th, she felt fine and encouraged me to leave for the hike. Once again Jim Simpson met me at the Table Rock Ranger's Station. I parked my car in the Table Rock State Park, and Jim transported me to the Foothills Trail western terminus at Oconee State Park. I started the hike at 11:30 a.m. and managed to hike 10.5 miles and camped for the evening along the Chattooga River.

On the next day, Friday I hiked 4.5 miles along the Chattooga River to the Burrell's Campground. I stopped and, had a snack for lunch at a picnic table. I then continued to hike to Fish Hatchery Road, and then the Sloan's Bridge Access. I arrived at 4:30 p.m. and decided to look for a camp spot on the way to the Whitewater Falls. I could not find an acceptable camp spot, so I continued to the Whitewater Falls and found a spot around 7 p.m. I certainly overextended myself today by hiking 18 miles. The sun had set and it began to rain as soon as I got my tent set. I skipped a hot dinner and just had a snack and laid down for a much needed rest.

The next morning I woke up early at 6:30 a.m. It was still very dark and cold approximately 50 degrees. I gathered my gear and left camp around 7:30 p.m. By this time the sun was rising and the sky was turning bright. I returned a very short distance to NC 281, which I had crossed last night, and took a spur trail along the road to the Upper Whitewater Falls parking lot and rest room. I stopped at a picnic table and cooked the hot dinner that I was supposed to have eaten last night and instead ate it for breakfast. After breakfast I used the rest room and then hiked to the end of the parking lot where there was a path to the Whitewater Falls overlook. The scenery was beautiful. I then descended at least 200 steps to a lower viewing platform. From this platform another set of steps led to the Foothills Trail and eventually descended into the gorge of the Whitewater River. At this point I crossed a 60 foot steel bridge and headed to the Duke Energy Bad Creek Access. After passing the Access the Foothills Trail ascended up a steep incline to a designated campsite on the peak of the mountain. I decided to try to call my wife and let her know I was all right. Cell service was very sparse along this trail, so usually when I got to a higher elevation I turned on my phone to check and see if I had service. I did have sevice and called her. I found out that she was not feeling well and that she wanted me to return home as soon as I could. Well, I felt disappointed once again by not completing my thru-hike. I called Jim Simpson and asked him to pick me up at the Duke Energy Bad Creek Access so I could return home. My total hike for this my second attempt was 32.3 miles.

It's all about the Journey

CHAPTER THREE - THE THIRD TIME IS A CHARM

October 19, 2017 – (Friday) I departed my home in Fort Mill, SC at 6:30 a.m. and arrived at the Table Rock State Park at 9:45 a.m. I met up with Jim Simpson at the Table Rock Ranger Office and Visitors Center. Once again I registered to thru- hike the Foothills Trail and obtained a car pass to park inside the Park for seven days while hiking the Trail. The registration served to notify the Rangers that I was hiking the trail and approximately when I would return. Jim followed me into the Park where I parked my car and after transferring my backpack to his truck we began our trip for the Oconee State Park 55 miles away. Throughout the hour and a half ride he pointed out scenic sites and markers where the Foothills Trail is located and intersected road crossings.

We arrived at the trailhead in the Oconee State Park at 11:15 a.m. After taking a few pictures at the trailhead sign, and thanking Jim once again for the ride, for the third time, I began my thru-hike. The first six miles of the trail to SC 107 crossing, and leaving the Oconee State Park was in very nice condition, relatively flat with only a few elevation changes. The trail was heavily wooded and lined with mountain laurel. After crossing SC 107 it was a short two mile hike mostly downhill to the Licklog Falls. The water over the falls was very abundant making the falls a beautiful sight. Leaving the falls the trail ascended up reasonably steep probably 300 or 400 feet in elevation for several miles and then descended down to the Chattooga River. Hiking another half mile or so I found a very nice camp site next to the river. After my dinner it began to get a little cool so I retired in my tent for a good night's sleep. The weather today was very sunny with a high of 65 degrees and I hiked for about 10½ miles.

October 20th – (Saturday) I left my camping site on the Chattooga River around 8:30 a.m. The 4.5 mile hike to the Burrell's Ford along the river was a very tough hike. The trail diverged from the river uphill in 5 different places. These inclines were very steep and took a path away from the river and eventually returned to the river. For the most part these diversions were caused by deep gorges that had to be passed around. The trail along the river was very narrow with lots of roots and eroded washouts and many up's and down's. Because it was the weekend there were many day hikers today on the trail and the narrow places made it very difficult to pass. When arriving at the Burrell's Ford Campground Parking lot I found there was a reward of a "Pit toilet". Of course I took advantage of this reward and then continued on my hike. Hiking out of the Burrell's Ford there was a steep 800 ft. rise up to the summit of the Medlin Mtn. There were several nice scenic vistas facing south on this stretch of the trail. As I continued to hike I passed through beautiful thickets of very large pine trees. From this point the trail followed on top of a ridge to the Fish Hatchery Road Access. After crossing the road the trail descended down several hundred feet and followed along a stream with several distant waterfalls. Eventually, I came up on the Sloan Bridge Access and decided to camp for the evening on a nice flat campsite just before the access. Close by was also a nice clear brook for me to both pump and filter water for my hydration reservoir and cooking dinner. There were several nice picnic tables at the access so I brought my food and stove up to one of the tables and enjoyed the comforts of home. The weather today was beautiful sunny and warm. I hiked 13.5 miles today with a total of 24 trail miles completed.

October 21st – (Sunday) Since I left home the weather prediction for Sunday evening and all day Monday had been for continuous rain possibly up to 4 inches. I listened to my weather radio last night and the forecast was still for severe downpours starting at 8 p.m. Sunday night and continuing to late Monday afternoon with the possibilities of tornadoes in the area. Before leaving the Sloan Bridge picnic area there was another reward, a "Pit toilet" which I used. When I started my hike this morning the weather was very nice sunny and warm. This section from the Sloan Bridge to the Whitewater Falls was 4.5 mile. The terrain was mostly an upgrade crossing the SC/NC state line and had some nice views of the Bad Creek Reservoir and the Lake Jocassee. I have read that the Bad Creek Reservoir, like the Lake Jocassee is a man-made body of water created by Duke Energy. Both bodies of water have dams for hydroelectric power plant, and the barriers are used during peak power requirement times. When not being used to generate electricity, water is replaced in the lakes by reversing the generators and pumping water back up into the impoundments.

When I arrived at NC 281 I went north along the road for 800 feet to the Whitewater parking and restroom area. There was a trash receptacle so I took advantage of it and discarded three days worth of trash I had accumulated. "Less weight to carry". At the end of the parking area there was a path that led up to the overlook of the Whitewater Falls. There was an abundance of water flowing over the falls making them look very spectacular. Off to the right side of the overlook, there were several hundred wooden steps leading to a lower overlook. I went down the steps; and, at the lower overlook, there was a sign, followed by another set of wooden steps leading down to the Foothills Trail. The Trail was a very steep, rocky, and strenuous descent, over 1000 feet down in elevation to a boulder field and rapids of the Whitewater River. I then crossed a 60 foot steel bridge over the river and stepped onto the Duke Energy property. After one and a half miles, almost flat hike along the river, I came to the intersection of the Duke Energy Bad Creek Access Trail. The Foothills Trail turned left and ascended up a hill to a junction where a blue blazed side trail lead to the Lower Whitewater Falls. It was getting a little late so I bypassed the opportunity to see the lower falls and continued on the white blazed trail. It crossed the NC/SC state line and soon came to a 75 foot wooden bridge over the Thompson River. There were 3 or 4 nice camping sites on the east side of the bridge. It was almost 5 p.m. so I decided to pick out a camp spot to spend the night. Paying attention to the current weather forecast I intended to hunker down here and probably remained all day Monday to stay dry until the weather passed. I carefully sized up all the flat spots, keeping in mind to avoid any spot where water might pool under my tent or flow down the mountain and flood me out. Next to the campsite that I picked, there was a small stream flowing out of the mountain down a bed rock wall and running down to the Thompson River. It was a perfect place to obtain water for my evening meal. After dinner I put all my gear in my tent to keep it dry and crawled in myself around 7:30 p.m. It began to rain around 8 p.m. and continued to rain very hard all night. I listened to my weather radio and the predictions were for 3 to 4 inches of rain and tornadoes in this area. When I woke up at 7 a.m. it was still raining very hard. The rain continued all day and my tent began to take on water around the lower sidewalls down at the foot of my tent. I had a Thermo-rest mattress so I kept above any wetness. Staying in the tent all day was not a comfortable feat and I felt like one of those baby calves that the farmers put in a little house to keep them small for veal. I did have my radio to listen to and a book to read. It wasn't until 3 p.m. that the rain subsided and I was able to get out of my tent. I could not believe my eyes perceiving the amount of water flowing in the Thompson River and also down the mountain next to my tent. I went out part way on the bridge crossing the river. The river was overflowing its banks, very turbulent and racing downstream. It made me fully understand why a person cannot survive a flash flood. I was happy to be alive and survived the storm being down low in a gorge. After listening to my radio I found out that this area had received 4 to 5 inches of rain and luckily the tornadoes that touchdown were far to the east of me. Around 5 p.m. the sky opened up and the sun came out. What a welcome sight. The weather prediction for the rest of the week was wonderful, sunny with days in the low 60's and early morning temperatures in the mid 40's.

October 23rd – (Tuesday) I packed up my gear. My tent was still very wet. I shook it out and dried it as much as possible before packing it. I left the Thompson River campsite at 9:15 a.m. on a bright sunny day. The river was still running very fast but had receded somewhat. The hike out was straight up hill four hundred feet in elevation. The trail leveled out and eventually descended down to a .2 mile side trail to the Hilliard Falls. After observing the falls I returned and soon crossed the Bearcamp Creek on a 35 foot wooden bridge. I continued for another four miles crossing a third wooden bridge and then got on an old logging road for 2.5 mile. At the end of the logging road there were steep wooden steps to the 115 foot wooden bridge over the Horsepasture River. A mile or so further I crossed a 50 foot suspension bridge over a dry gorge and continued to the Bear Creek Campground by crossing yet another 35 foot bridge after which I stopped in a large campground for lunch. After lunch I re-crossed the same 35 foot bridge and continued on the Foothills Trail for another six miles passing under high voltage power lines and into a section called the Cross Cobb Creek. This section was simply beautiful. It reminded me of a tropical garden with a very rare plant that only grew in this area called "Oconee Bell". They lined both sides of the trail like ground covers. At the base of this area there was a stone pathway that extended along and over a clear running brook. The trail then ascended out of this area, crossed another stream on two timbers, and began a steep one mile descend into the Lake Jocassee shores. I crossed a 225 foot suspension bridge over the Toxaway River and stepped into the Gorges State Park. There were many excellent campsites with picnic tables so I chose a beautiful site overlooking the Lake Jocassee for my night's stay. My hike today was 14.1 miles and a total 48.5 trail miles from the Oconee State Park.

October 24th – (Wednesday) I hiked out of the Lake Jocassee area around 9 a.m. It was cold this morning around 40 degrees but sunny. The trail took me to 100s and 100s of wooden steps up the "Heartbreak Ridge". As soon as I reached the summit there were 100's of wooden steps that took me back down to the forest floor. The next 5.8 miles to the Laurel Fork Falls were very scenic and included lots of wooden steps both up and down. There were also sections where the trail took to old logging roads making my hiking like a simple "walk in the woods". When I approached the Laurel Fork Falls overlook I discovered it was simply beautiful. There was an abundant amount of water flowing over the fall probably from the rain storm on Monday. I followed the trail a short distance and crossed over the Laurel Fork Creek on a 75 foot suspension bridge. On the other side there was a very large camping area where I stopped to have lunch. On my afternoon hike I passed the Virginia Hawkins Falls that was also beautiful but it was less than half the size of the Laurel Fork Falls. Continuing I ascended out of the Laurel Fork Creek Valley by once again climbing many wooden steps. Hiking several miles further I came upon a designated flat open camping area at mile 59.1 and camped for the evening. It was another premium fall sunny day. Today's hike was 10.6 miles.

October 25th – (Thursday) It was another beautiful morning. It was very sunny and a little warmer this morning than yesterday. Today I hoped to hike over the summit of the Sassafras Mountain, the highest point in South Carolina. I left the 59.1 mile camping site at 9 a.m. It was only three miles to the Laurel Valley Access parking lot at SC 178. This would be another "milestone" for me for this was where I had to leave the Foothills Trail on my first thru-hike attempt. My hike this morning started out with a steep descent of many wooden steps to Horsepasture Road and then an ascent up wooden steps to an old level logging road, which more or less ran parallel 50 to 60 feet above Horsepasture Road. As I hiked along I could hear hunters' hound dogs tracking the scent of a black bear. I also saw several hunters in white trucks passing below. The hunting season for bear must have opened up a few days ago. Yesterday when I was hiking on and above Schoolhouse Road, I met up with hunters in their all terrain vehicles tracking their dogs. The presence of the hunters and dogs did not make me feel comfortable while in the same section of the woods. The only saving grace was that both yesterday and today I had not heard any gunfire.

As I crossed SC 178 I felt a small sense of achievement by beginning to explore an uncharted section of the Foothills Trail that I had not hiked. The trail ahead of me to the summit of the Sassafras Mountain is a 4.4 mile climb and a gain of 1850 vertical feet. The hike up was very steep with many switchbacks. It took me almost 4 hours. Upon reaching the summit there was a beautiful 360 degree view of the Blue Ridge Mountains of the Appalachian Mountain Chain. There is a stone monument on the summit with a Brass Plaque that reads, "Sassafras Mountain elevation 3553 feet". "This plaque marks the highest point in the state of South Carolina". I met a man on the summit who was tracking migrating birds. While talking with him he pointed out distance points of interest such as the Mount Mitchell the tallest mountain east of the Mississippi River, the Mount Pisgah and also almost the entire length of the Blue Ridge Parkway in North Carolina. I began my descend at 3 p.m. and had a 5 mile hike to Drawbar Cliffs, a large rock outcrop where there was a small camp site I wanted to stay at tonight. On my way down the Sassafras Mountain I stopped by a place called the Chimney Remains at the John L Cantrell home site. I saw the remains of an old chimney and scattered stones, which were probably a part of the Cantrell's cabin many years ago. There were several very neat campsites nearby with a large fire pit that had ten stone chairs around it. The chairs were probably built with the remains of the chimney stones and were all formed like lounge chairs including backrests and armrests. I was incredibly impressed for I have never seen anything like this arrangement throughout all my hiking experiences. I even tried sitting in several of them and they were very comfortable. As I continued on for a few more miles I finally arrived at my campsite for the evening. Today had been another beautiful day, in which I hiked 12 miles and now at a total of 71.1 miles from the Oconee State Park.

October 26th – (Friday) "Completion Day". When I started off this morning I only had a little over 5 miles to the Table Rock State Park terminus of the Foothills Trail. After hiking 1000 feet or so I came to a beautiful camping site with a scenic view overlooking the Lake Keowee and surrounding towns. I felt bad realizing that last night I had missed this camping opportunity. As I continued I eventually arrived at a sign that pointed towards a steep side trail to the summit of Pinnacle

Mountain. I dropped my pack and left it by the sign while taking the .3 mile trail to the summit. When I arrived I found there was no vista, just a sign indicating the summit with an elevation of 3425 feet. On the way down I passed another sign that indicated it was "Bald Knob". Here was a beautiful vista of the South Carolina Foothills looking south. The remainder of my hike to the Table Rock State Park was all downhill passing quite a few day hikers once again being the beginning of the weekend. Close to the terminus there were several small waterfalls, a steel bridge, and a wooden causeway that brought me to the parking lot where my Mini Cooper had been patiently waiting for me. I drove it up to the upper campgrounds restroom and took a very long well needed hot shower and got dressed in clean clothes for my trip back home.

CHAPTER FOUR – LESSONS LEARNED WHILE ON THE FOOTHILLS

The Foothills Trail is a very fun and challenging hiking trail to thru-hike. It is an excellent hike both for experienced hikers as well as the beginner overnighters. It has a very diverse terrain including plenty of water sources and camping opportunities. Matter of fact it has so many water sources I did not find it necessary to carry any more than one liter of water during the day while hiking the entire length of the trail. There are no shortages of interesting sights to see or vistas to be inspired by. With its entire rivers, streams, and brooks, many waterfalls, scenic overlooks and vistas, my hike every day was captivated with excitement almost hourly. I was fascinated and amazed with all the incredible styles and number of bridges that crossed its many rivers, streams, brooks and gorges. The trail was well maintained, well marked, and had diversities of its terrain between ascents and descents. I totally enjoyed my thru-hiking of this trail and highly recommend it to any devoted backpacker. I found the entire length of the trail to be very neat and clean with very few sightings of litter. I cannot say enough praise about the Foothills Trail Conference. Their website and publications were very helpful but most of all, the dedication of the volunteer shuttle drivers were much appreciated.

My only recommendation to the Foothills Trail Conference for future improvements is to consider installing shelters or lean-to's in some of its designated campground sites and also installing decomposing privies. With the amount of traffic that the Foothills Trail receives this would enhance safety during inclement weather and improve cleanliness around the perimeters of the designated camping areas.

Jim Simpson my dedicated Shuttle Driver

Oconee State Park – Terminus of the Foothills Trail – Mile 0

It's all about the Journey

Chattooga River – Mile 12

Narrow Trail along Chattooga River-Mile-15

Sloan Bridge Access (where I camped close-by) Mile 23.9

Vista of Lake Jocassee – Mile 26.9

It's all about the Journey

The Beautiful Whitewater Falls – Mile 29

One of many sets of steps along the Trail

Whitewater River Lower Gorge – Mile 30

Steel bridge crossing Whitewater River

Thompson River before the Storm – Mile 34.4

Thompson River after 6 inches of rainfall

Thompson River Camp Site where I hunkered down for two days

Thompson River camp site after Sunday's and Monday's rain storm

Time out for a bath in Bearcamp Creek –Mile-37

Success on the Foothills Trail

Bridge over Horsepasture River – Mile 40.2

50 ft. suspension bridge over dry ravine – Mile 41.3

Foothills Trail passes under the high tension power lines - Mile 43.6

Cross Cobb Creek area with Oconee Bell plants lacing the trail – Mile 44.9

Cross Cobb Creek stepping stones

225 foot suspension bridge over the Toxaway River – Mile 48.5

Toxaway River cuts deep into the gorge

Picturesque Lake Jocassee

Campsite at Laurel Fork Falls in Gorges State Park – Mile 49

The beautiful Laurel Fork Falls – Mile 54.3

Foothills Trail crosses SC 178 – Mile 62

Steep 4.2 mile climb up to the summit of Sassafras Mtn.

Plaque at the summit of Sassafras Mountain – Mile 66.4

View from the summit of Sassafras Mountain

Northeast view from Sassafras Mountain

Stone seats around the campfire pit at Chimney Remains – Mile 67.6

Success on the Foothills Trail

View from Bald Knob near summit of Pinnacle Mtn. – Mile 72.5

Wooden Causeway at Table Rock State Park terminus – Mile 76.2

"The Final Reward," Swimming Beach at Table Rock State Park close to the terminus of the Foothills Trail

It's all about the Journey

About the Author

Richard T. Monahan has been hiking, backpacking, and camping along the Appalachian Mountain Chain since he was 69 years old. He is in the Class of 2015 thru-hikers of the Appalachian Trail. The following year he authored *End To End in Seven Section Hikes, Quality Time Spent on the Appalachian Trail*. Originally from New England he now lives in South Carolina where he continues to hike many backcountry trails in the Blue Ridge Mountain Chain.

Made in the USA
Middletown, DE
12 August 2018